Wonder Electric

Wonder Electric

Poems by

Elizabeth Cohen

Cover design by Shay Culligan

ISBN: 978-1-954353-57-2

Kelsay Books
502 South 1040 East, A-119
American Fork, Utah, 84003

Acknowledgments

Gracious acknowledgment is given to the following publications, where these poems first appeared:

Adanna Literary Journal: "The Watch," "The Waiting"
Bullets-to-Bells website: "Deer Season"
Crosswinds Journal: "Mowing"
Pangolin Review: "Something, not the other thing," "The Possible"
Persephone's Daughters: "Daughter's Onomatopoeia"
Poor Yorick: "Bernie Sanders is on My Daughter's Flight to New York City"

Gratitude to Samme Chittum & Brad Torum for "The Eddy"; to Michael Faris for 2nd Avenue; appreciation is also given here to Dara-Lyn Schrager for her keen editorial eye, and finally, to the Wonder Electric company of Wonder Valley, for the use of their sign image.

Contents

Wonder Electric

In the walls of the house
spirits are shuffling,
check out their powers
to heat water, make toast

send strips of light
running into the yard,
painting the dark
when the tiniest deer approach.

And how the whole kitchen
illuminates when you
open the refrigerator door,
a phosphorescent glow

from that ethereal shrine,
humming once an hour,
protecting soup
manchego, the guacamole.

Here, in this republic
of tamed energy, you can read
by pointed ghost-light,
you can sew

by Tiffany campfire—
each moon-tug on the earth
makes a tide that could heat
a bath, each breeze could blow

water into steam.
Soon, they say, even the axis
of north and south
will throw

down their magnetic dice.
Imagine—everything backwards
and upside down and the children,
everywhere, watching the show.

Mowing

Decapitating the lilac heads of the clover,
purring over a soft fold of mushroom caps,
the jackhammer push over a few stray stones
toward this goal: the lawn's trim locks,
the way the azaleas pop, freed from fringe

Those fresh tendrils spent their whole lives waving to us,
the last butter-soft dandelion froth floats away,
the reverse of snow. Later, a baby crow sucked
into the pool skimmer, blue-black feathers brined
in chorine; a single black eye staring up
through the sprinkler rainbow

The dead want to tell us something they know:
Nothing is something too, they say
When it is July and we are unemployed and sick,
hungry enough to see even nothing wants a glass of water
even nothing can have a relapse.
Even nothing needs a rest.

Brahms During Plague

No matter where you are
no matter what you are doing
or what the weather report
or the surgeon general
have to say, there is always a celebration
of violins in D Major happening
somewhere; a sonorous conversation
between strings and bassoons,
a congregation of grace notes with delicate
crescendos of cymbal and bass drum
right there—under the wingspan
of every moment, every day.

No matter what the date,
even on the anniversaries of dead lovers
and Hiroshima, tsunamis,
and days your oldest relatives recall
of far too much rain, there is always
one muscular phrase climbing
onto the back of another for a ride,
day in, day out, during wars,
holidays, on the birthday
of your firstborn.

Even on the day the last iceberg
calves from what's left
of Greenland, or the poles,
you can be assured that a single violin's voice
will be rising, with so much to say
about how centuries can pass along
hard beauty, even in difficult weather,
one note at a time.

Spring, and This

despite the fact that it is the most beautiful weather
despite the fact that the road
has been freed from construction

despite that last link of a rainbow saluting
us from the cloud perimeter

despite all this and the azaleas' velvet faces
the whales have decided to die

old whales and mother whales and their calves
have thrown themselves onto the beach, lump
like silver hills over children's sand forts

the territory parents have staked out
with umbrellas and cotton duck sea chairs

despite the candidates lined up
like pageant contestants
tap-dancing their best promises

the whales have cast their ballots:
no—to deep-sea currents
no—to zooplankton and krill

no—to the intercontinental shelf
spiraled with reef-light-tortoise-migrations

the whales are dying, and a group of people
are trying to push them back into the sea
someone found a YouTube video on their phone

but it isn't working—these particular whales
are too large and too serious about their dying

it is clear by the way they are stacked
all the way to the concession stand that dying
is what they have decided to do today

there has been a disagreement on their precise genus
someone insists pilot, no, beluga, no, blue

people are taking pictures; Channel 2 has arrived,
they are filming, and people are gathering to watch
despite the excellent weather forecast, despite the children

who were so well-behaved in the car and despite
the fact that this was a very good week for the stock market

the whales are dying. In the hot sun, they blister and poach
a white dog in a red sweater is barking at them

a very small girl in a yellow bathing suit has made her way
to the side of the bull, she reaches her hand out
to touch before her grandmother snaps her away

Deer Season

Early Bow

single note of release
in the autumn fire-spice wind
shadow lace buck droppings
the final sunflowers falling down
spilled mustard on the path

Crossbow

over the loon hills
they find the shy ones
hiding

Youth hunt

chewing gum, boot crunch
wrinkle wrappers untethered
sunrise in the whisper thick
dusk and still coming hard even after
against regulations

Muzzleloader

scent of black steam powder
distant reports
shudder and holler out the valley news

Regular season

but then, what is "regular"?
a solemn tree speaking to the moss
funeral dirge for the doe
pierced open and spilling
guts, blood, and the remains
of an unborn fawn, half-eaten by crows

Adirondack early season

for the deer, obviously, it is *always* deer season:
season for shadow napping; nibble and pivot season,
breeding season, season for birthing in the tree-deep brush
ripe berries season and first-grass-carpet-grazing-stealing-roots
season, it is always leap year for deer, sipping from rain pockets
on the leaves

Semi-automatic

by the time you read this, it will be happening somewhere else
the shutter quick splatter shots
spraying down of the whole of everything
first step to wedding vows, the wheelchair ones
teenagers in their sweats and bralettes
it is always open semi-automatic season in America
the moon blinks back, half or full, new or
blood, black or harvest, it watches
like a torn eye

AK-47

you got Marcy, you got Stephen
you got baby Anders
you got the whole Smith family
out for ice cream
you got them
you got you got you got you got you got got got got
spent cartridges on the floor of the bar, fair, synagogue
church, school, market, big-box store, each one a funeral
calling card with someone's name on it:
Marcus, Hunter, Riley, Ben, Serendipity
Dylan, Alan, Julia, Beatrice
names fall like leaves, flutter down
you know it's been AK-47 season when you see the names piling
up
and then, later, when they are swept away

Dogs Can Smell the Dark

In fourth grade, our teacher
told us dogs could smell darkness

and furthermore cancer
and that hospitals

sometimes bring them in
to help spot illness early on

it was remarkable
to think

those same animals that begged
for scraps and made chaos

of the trash at the skatepark
had such *abilities*

At home, our dogs
dug a hole

behind our father's rose garden
so deep he said

we could probably peer down
and see Antarctica

We used to listen to them howl
when the other dogs howled

in people's yards far away
thinking maybe they were telling

each other how to do it
or describing what darkness smells like

or furthermore, light

Imprints

These are the places we lay
on the sand.

You can still see us,
side by side,

the little wrinkles in
our clothing,

the place your sneaker
dug, making a trough.

We have left behind
the impressions of our feet,

both coming and departing,
each one a small boat

floating on a sand sea,
each one leaving somewhere

and arriving somewhere else,
further out. There are so many

other places we left evidence.
You could make a whole

compendium of our snow angels,
sleek runs and turns down mountains,

the crosshatched remains
our snowshoes-stamped

on mountainsides.
And the place, of course

where you are buried now,
that mounded spot

with its rough, sloping, granite stone,
and the place beside it, waiting for me.

The world is printed with us,
summer to spring.

We have left ourselves everywhere.
Our love litters the planet,

even blows like the escaped
plastic bags, moving over avenues

into deserts and northern forests,
where they'll catch sometimes, in the trees.

The Waiting

Sitting by a window
peering from the heavy bone sockets
of her eyes

this is my mother
in her last days
living on nibbled lamb

and grapefruit juice
feeding the last bits of summer
to a single bird

waiting for my father
down the hall, in a separate unit
of the New York State Veteran's Home

to come out
and greet her
which he never does

The Watch

This is the last of my mother's
many gold-plated watches—
a *Timex,* the sort you wind up
with an elastic band
that might catch on the small hairs
of your arm, an experience that provokes
a twinge, something not quite pain
but certainly not pleasant
not so unlike the feeling in your chest
each time you see this watch
still sitting on the bathroom shelf
all these years later
as if the ghost of her might
be wondering what time it is
or if she might step out of the shower
or wake from a nap
and think *where is my watch*
where is my daughter
where is my life

Full Moon in Taurus

hanging behind thundersnow
sometimes you have to reinvent your dreams
the good news: this can be done

keep a little chip of God in your pocket
this could be a rock you found
forty-seven years ago

your daughter's baby tooth
or the sand
still listing in your pocket

from that day at the beach
those tidal pools
you found so emblematic

and they were, you just didn't understand
yet how the water filling and un-filling the rocky scape
would answer a question
you had not yet asked

Lucky

That day I found a nickel
lodged between dawn and the curb
picked it up
(thinking to myself
what are the chances)

someone had to drop a nickel
right in that spot, and it probably rolled a little
then came winter
burying it in a whole agenda
of snowpack and boots

then in spring
my eyes had to be free
to slant toward the ground
when it reappeared
and it was lucky, too, that

I was even there as I was supposed
to be in New York at your funeral
but I missed that
as I had to work three jobs to pay
for the college trip

my daughter took into the dark heart
of the plague for which she was quarantined
after Milan, and took sick with fever
and lucky, really lucky, she lived
and further

that she was born in the first place
after the other one died 22 years earlier
right there in the taxi, just bled out
during rush hour in August, staining
the seat and even so the driver

was so kind I will always remember
how he took me to Saint Joseph's
and walked me in. It was lucky, I am lucky
I have a nickel

This Is How You Survive

Me with my lonely mama heart and my empty nest and my dreams of the west and my white gaze and my broken left foot and my unfinished novel and my reams of grading and my sick cat and my dog-who-needs-a-walk and my dead parents and my left-of-center politics and my carpal tunnel wrist and my broken heart and my overdue taxes and my love of trees and my last 50 dollars and my good socks and my darling nephew and my N-95 mask, and my flex spending account, and my balanced portfolio, and my recurring dream of ice, and my affection for birds, and my dusty ceiling fan, and my house needing paint, and my bandage of poetry when the night comes flying in, like a thrown knife.

Daughter's Onomatopoeia

If you could touch this poem
you might feel the hiss and spit of the sprinklers
in the yard outside or the tremulous way
I am sobbing
as I type it

If you could smell this poem
it would be the scent of frangipani shampoo
as I kiss the top of her head before she trips
away from the terrible, beautiful things her life
has branded upon her

Past the Eremurus Cleopatra stand, past the cracks
in the pavement, past the whole bloom and tick
of summer and the brittle twigs from when we sliced
back the hydrangeas, that last time we ever
worked together on the yard
or, for that matter, on anything

Bernie Sanders Is on My Daughter's Flight to NYC

she is headed for Israel
he is on his way to the first presidential debate
in Miami. she is wearing leggings and an oversized
sweater, he has on a rumpled suit
they both have seats in economy
sunshine makes a grid on the terminal carpet
igniting big plate glass windows that face the runway
which I face as I sit on one of those rocking chairs
in the Burlington Airport to answer her text
Yes, I saw him. Yes. Yes. He looks good.
It is true. Bernie Sanders is on the same plane
as my daughter. He has lost some weight.
we remark upon his general well-being
and his ordinariness. he is just a man
running for president, after all
in about thirty minutes they will both be served
drinks and little packages of sweet biscuits and
peanuts. later, each will roll their carry-ons
to their next destinations, and the future
will roll back toward them as well
towing its brute baggage of horror
the ramping up of respirator manufacture
and a run on surgical masks, in which somewhere
in Italy a nurse will look over a dozen beds
and make a decision every hour
but all this has not yet happened.
the plane fits so nicely in the blue sky
winks in the early sun then soars with silvery grace
like the great blue heron we saw on Grand Island
on the drive to the airport

the firmament parting for it, the gentle rise beyond
the tree line. the plate glass trembles slightly
and I notice my hand is trembling, too
and I feel the force of the future
bearing down, sometimes you can sixth sense that

and on this day it is leaden
full of the possibility of all things rushing forward
beautiful and raw, and all the cemeteries
with their slack maws and bulldozers
waiting for the living to become the dead

The Possible

It is winter in Plattsburgh, New York
Each day closes in on itself
like a drawer

There is an essential mystery
about how things arrived here
the close walls, the unfinished paint

The lost loves
their scattered gifts on shelves
some still in their boxes

All the world just sitting
in this house that is merely a gap in the snow
a not-snowy caesura, breeding dust

There was a time when this was different,
the good bones of the house
historic columns

The swimming pool
like a hopeful blue eye
the sunny room of plants

But the girl grew up, the dog died,
the other dog that came
chewed on the heels of the couch

All morning, the possible rages around the house
like a pandemic, the afternoon resembling a letter
which was actually an unopened invitation

forgotten in a book in a drawer
The snow wraps everything in mummy cloth
preserving the white forgivable margin

Something, Not the Other Thing

If you love something, let it go. If it comes back to you, it must have had some sort of invisible tether or maybe it owed you money or remembered it left something of value at your house. A totally different tactic is to put it in a bottle, add in attractive pebbles, feed it sunflower seeds and cardamom buns, dampen it with holy water, tell it riddles until it weeps

But best of all would be to take this loved thing to the model train exhibit at the New Mexico state fair, read it Blake and cook it pasta Caccio e Pepe; give it a seaweed wrap with lavender oil to draw out toxins and break up the waste in its lymphatic system. Any of these would probably do the trick, which is to get that loved thing to be a part of the world you inhabit forever, so it can slay your loneliness and just stay

The End

—For Christopher

the thing about the end
is it is a lot like the beginning
you have your coffee; you start your car
you drive somewhere
you read a newspaper

everything follows the expected map of your days
the fallen snow disguises the garbage
laid out to be taken away
someone is shoveling, and the sound
is the same scrape and huff as ever

you put a bandage on a small cut
you feed the cats, walk the dog
all the while knowing that deep down
everything is different now

you are different
and before you is a book you have
not yet opened, full of pages of fire
and earth, water and air
and light, infinite light

About the Author

Elizabeth Cohen is a poet. She is the author of the chapbook *The Economist's Daughter* and two books of poetry, *Bird Light* and *The Patron Saint of Cauliflower.* Her poems have been published in *River Styx, Northwest Review, Tiferet Journal, Hawaii Review, Kalliope, Yale Review, NYU Black Renaissance Noire, Exquisite Corpse,* and other literary journals, as well as in *Walk on the Wild Side: Urban American Poetry Since 1975,* among other anthologies.

Her memoir, *The Family on Beartown Road,* was an NYT Notable Book of the Year, and her book of short stories, *The Hypothetical Girl,* was awarded the Best Fiction Book of 2017 by the Adirondack Center for Writing. She has taught Creative Writing at Western Connecticut State University, Binghamton University, and The University of New Mexico Gallup Extension as well as through Gotham Writer's Workshops. She is an associate professor of English at SUNY Plattsburgh.